# Strong W.O.M.A.N. The Mini-Book

# Strong W.O.M.A.N. The Mini-Book

A PRACTICAL GUIDE TO
OVERCOMING OBSTACLES
USING THE QUALITIES OF GOD
IN YOU

## Dr. Cheryl Edwards Buckingham, PhD

Thus Said Productions LLC

# Contents

1. Preface — 1
2. Acknowledgements — 3
3. Highlights of My Story — 6
4. WOMAN — 14
5. W—Wisdom — 16
6. O—Overcomer — 21
7. M—Modesty — 29
8. A—Anointing — 34
9. N—Nurturer — 40
10. STRONG W.O.M.A.N. — 44

*references* — 49

Copyright © 2021 by Dr. Cheryl Edwards Buckingham, PhD

All rights reserved. No part of this book may be reproduced in any manner whatsoever without written permission except in the case of brief quotations embodied in critical articles and reviews.

First Printing, 2021

# 1

## Preface

The writing of this mini-book began about nine years ago (circa 2011). I felt there was a message God wanted to get to his daughters, that would aid in spiritual strengthening. This book details qualities and characteristics that a Strong Woman should exude and continue to develop. Each chapter discusses a character trait that God wants his Strong Women to walk in and live by. The journey to writing this book was not an easy one. Through the tests and trials that I have endured and overcome as a woman, wife, mother, daughter, sister, and friend, God has developed me in the areas of this book and equipped me to be able write about these traits and areas to help guide women. My hope is that women will walk away more knowledgeable, encouraged, and empowered to live in victory, enjoy life, and not let life's challenges and pitfalls keep them down. Don't let despair, hatred, bitterness, unforgiveness, depression, or sadness keep you from having victory in life.

The publication of this book has allowed me to truly see God has everything worked out and a plan for it all. I encourage you to keep believing and dreaming. Dream, Girl! Happy Reading!

# 2

## *Acknowledgements*

There are lots of people who have been instrumental to me in the writing of this mini-book. Thank you to my husband, Daniel Buckingham Sr., for your patience and continued nudge to push me to get the mini-book done, and not sit on the assignment that God had given me. Sometimes I didn't want to hear it, but I needed to hear it. Thank you for backing me, reassuring me, and encouraging me. Thank you to my parents, Frank and Rita Eaton, for a lifetime of love and support in all my endeavors. Thank you, Mom, for being the best mother that a daughter could ever dream of having. Thank you, Dad for your sacrifices and being our contingency plan when we needed it. Mom and Dad, I am thankful for all your hard work in ensuring that your girls were taken care of and for being a foundation for our family. Thank you to my sister, Crystal Maryland, for being there for me and being supportive through it all (the good, the bad, and the ugly).

Thank you to my sister Latanya Tyler for a lifetime of love shown. Thank you to my Aunt Mona Shelton and Aunt Yvonne Hudson, for being like second moms and always being caring, supportive and present. Thank you to my Uncle Wallace Shelton for your consistent support. Thank you to my Aunt Mary Eaton for your compassion and love. Thank you to my Aunt Yolanda Edwards for your love. Thank you to my Uncle Hyman Lee Edwards, Aunt Betty Williams, and Aunt Delilah Brown for showing love. Thank you to my Mother-in-law Dianne Crews for your steadfast support, assurance, and love. Thank you to my Sister-in-law Ronda Westbrook for always supporting me and being a listening ear over the last twenty-plus years. Thank you to my Sister-in-law Charla Williams for your support. Thank you to my Niece Tria Hamiel for being one of my beta readers and for being the advocate that you are. Thank you to my Nephew Troy Coles for assisting with graphic design and layout. Thank you to my Crews family, for your love and support in our endeavors: Michelle, Bobby, Darrell, Kevin, Sty, Nikisha, Andrea, Aunt Iris, Aunt Cynthia, Apostle Rose, and Apostle Doris. Thank you to my Buckingham family, for your love and support in our endeavors: Grandma Henrietta, Aunt Lucille, Aunt Jackie, Aunt Sheila, Uncle Melvin, Aunt Tangie, Elaine, Mary and Barbara Harris. Thank you to Reverend Dr. Janet K. Copeland for your mothering and spiritual mentorship. Thank you to Minister Wilfred and Mother Robin Tyree for your support. Thank you to Elders Donald and Yolanda Ross of For Better or For Worse Ministry, for being a champion for marriages. Thank you to my friend Tanra Easter for your prayers and support. Thank you to friend Cortney Knapp for your support and positivity. Thank you to friend Shannon Vincent for our early morning talks and for being a beta reader. Thank you to friend First Lady Tamara Green Jones for being a beta reader and giving me the feedback that I needed. Thank you to my always supportive friend Dr. Natalie Moss Gooden, for being a beta reader, as well as championing me/us, and being my accountability partner, when I needed it the most. To my oldest goddaughter Brianna, thank you for including me in all your milestones, it means the world to me. I am tremendously proud of you. I am extremely grateful for my sons, Daniel Jr. and Christopher, who motivate and inspire me to keep pushing towards my daily and long-term goals, as I continue to evolve into my best self. I would like to posthumously thank and honor, my Grandma (Ganny) Christine Smith and my favorite cousins growing up, Angela LaDawn Monroe and Latisha Charita Harris.

There are also several Pastors whose ministries, assistance, and prayers have been substantial to my spiritual growth and development: Dr. Gene and Lady Barbara Donaldson, Pastor Steve Parson, Bishop Lloyd and Pastor Pamela Westbrook, Pastor Michael and Pastor Raquel Maye, Reverend Dr. Lois Bias, and Spiritual Parents Pastor Fred and Pastor Inger Wyatt of Speaking Spirit Ministries (Richmond, Virginia).

# 3

## Highlights of My Story

I've grown up around church most of my life. My earliest memories of church were during my elementary school years, going to "the little white church," that sat on top of the hill in Southside Richmond, near Hillside Court housing projects. I remember us learning about God and singing songs like "This Little Light of Mine." I remember going to church with Momma Sharon (a family friend) and seeing her play the piano and be active in the church. I remember going to Easter egg hunts with the neighborhood kids. When my parents purchased a home and moved to the East End, my church experiences continued. From Mt. Olivet Baptist Church and 31st Street Baptist with my childhood friends to Cedar Street Baptist and Faith Community Baptist Church with my aunts. I have so many fond memories of Sunday School, Vacation Bible School, and riding the church van. Little did I know, God was building a foundation within me.

When I visited my maternal grandmother, I would also attend church with her. She was more of a Southern Baptist. In my teen years, I joined and attended Ephesus Seventh-day Adventist (SDA) Church with my parents and sisters. My maternal great grandma was a devout SDA, and my dad attended Ephesus Junior Academy as a youngster. While at Ephesus, I was involved in youth programs, ushered, and loved spending time with the First Lady of the church and her daughter. I learned a lot about Christ, and God continued to mold me during those years.

When I went off to college at the University of Mary Washington (then Mary Washington College), I was faced with lots of choices and freedoms that most freshmen away from home experience. Because of the foundation that had already been developed within me, I didn't go "buck wild," even though I was miles away from home and my parents. My college experiences were filled with great memories of friends and our adventures and mishaps. That's not to say there weren't tests, trials, temptations, learning experiences, and failures along the way—because there were! One of the lasting learning experiences I had was learning about credit card debt. As a teenager in high school, this was never a real focus in Business classes. In college students are offered credits cards almost as often as they are offered food. I took the bait and got my first credit card. I didn't use the credit card for lots of frivolous things, but I did use it for supplies, dorm items, car items, clothes, and fun activities. I quickly realized that my job as a Resident Assistant wasn't going to cut it to pay off the debt I had amassed. During my summers I worked as a Nursing Assistant and took summer classes, to lessen my loads during regular semesters. My parents were also able to help me, which was a Godsend. That was a difficult lesson to endure and a lesson that I can now pass on to my children and other youth so that they don't make the same mistake.

There were other challenges and decisions that I made in college that I think prevented me from later hardships. Even though I went to a few clubs with my friends, I never allowed myself to be open to certain destructive behaviors while in those environments. I was never inebriated to the point of making irrational decisions. I never invited unknown people to visit me in my private living space. When I travelled alone, to run errands or sightsee, in Northern Virginia and DC, I was always aware of my surroundings.

Amid college life and finding a balance between academics, campus life, and social life, I also became involved in lots of student organizations including the Black Student Association, Women of Color, programs with the Multicultural Center, Voices of Praise (a gospel choir), and the Campus Christian Community Center (CCC). The CCC was an organization that conducted church services for students, community service events, and social activities. The CCC was considered an ecumenical student ministry (nondenominational, interdenominational, universal), supported by several Methodist, Presbyterian, Lutheran, and Episcopal churches. Several of my friends and I had fun and interesting times at the CCC. In sharing these experiences, I am sharing some highlights of how God and church have been an ongoing part of my life.

I met my now husband during the fall of my senior year of college. We became friends and dated. After graduating from college, I returned to home to start a career and "adult." In returning,

I visited and attended multiple churches from Ephesus to St. Paul's Baptist Church. Looking back, I now realize that internally, I was on a quest for a deeper experience and relationship with God. Fast-forward a few years, my husband and I married, and he introduced me to Richmond Christian Center (RCC), where my mother in law was a faithful member. It was at RCC where I received the holy spirit with the evidence of speaking in tongues.

Fast-forward a few more years (this is a mini-book), time moved on, and the stages of life continued. During this time in my life, I was married, working for a Fortune 500 company, had finished a master's degree program, and had a young son. It was during this time frame that issues begin to arise within my marriage, from arguments to communication issues, poor decision making and money mishandling. As a result, there were financial losses, a home foreclosure, backlash from family and friends, and a sense of diminished dignity. When situations like these arise in a marriage or a relationship, the human-natured response is offense, anger, rage, and thoughts of self-preservation. The "we" turns into "I" and "me." To overcome this state and the situation, I had to turn to God and rely on God. What does that really mean? We hear people say this all the time. It means speaking the word of God (actual Bible verses that are applicable and relevant) over your situations, and knowing that based on Proverbs 18:21, life and death, success and failure are in the power of the tongue (what you say out of your mouth). Speaking the word out loud enables us to overcome and to fight against disbelief and doubt that may try to creep in. In order to know what the word of God says, so that you can speak it, you have to read it and/or listen to it. My journey to overcome and mend my marriage and relationships involved reading the word of God, fasting to break through barriers and strongholds, not giving my ear (listening) to others or allowing them to speak against what I believed God for (which was a healthy marriage and family), and praising and worshipping God in the midst of waiting for change. I purchased CDs of my favorite praise and worship songs and artists, that were able to minister to my soul through their songs, and I praised and worshipped as I was going through situations I thought would break me.

One vivid memory I have was dancing in the family room of my house, which was in the basement. During this time, there was a lot of household discord between my husband and me, and I felt angry, confused, and disappointed. I remember turning on praise music, blasting the speakers, and just dancing and praising until I actually praised myself happy. I didn't think that was even possible. As I praised and worshiped and danced, it felt like negativity and burdens were being lifted. When I was done, I was tired, but I felt better inside and was able to push on. The overcoming process also required walking in love and forgiveness, not holding onto offenses, as well as letting go of hurts, failures, and disappointments. One of God's greatest commandments, in the Bible, is to love. How can you show love and spread love if you continue to hold onto offenses and hurt, which can turn into bitterness, resentment, or hatred? Ephesians 4:31-32 says, "Let all bitterness and wrath and anger and clamor and slander be put away from you, along with all malice. Be kind to one another, tenderhearted, forgiving one another, as God in Christ forgave you." Holding onto unforgiveness can hinder God answering your prayers or moving on your behalf.

Over the span of the last ten years plus, the situations

that my husband and I endured and persevered through include household financial collapse, struggling to purchase necessities, cars having mechanical issues and not knowing how they would be fixed, marital arguments, and going through a foreclosure. Losing our house in foreclosure and starting over was a huge blow. My husband and I lived apart for a few months, as we decided what would be next. Through all of this, we decided we were not going to let the enemy win and the enemy was not going to destroy what God had put together. The rebuilding process was not an easy one. I know what it means when you hear people say you've had more month than money. There were times when nights were sleepless, when anxiety and worry tried to creep in. All the while I was putting on a courageous face for my oldest son, not showing my disappointment at the time and putting on a smile and good cheer for Corporate America while my home life was in disorder and uncertainty. There were moments of anger, rage, and even self-doubt. During these times, I did not allow anger, rage, bitterness, unforgiveness, or self-doubt to stay. I prayed and interceded, I praised and worshipped even when I didn't "feel" like it or when it didn't "feel" like anything was happening or changing, and I fasted. I took a stand against the enemy and declared that he could not and would not have my family. Once I began to do my part, it allowed God to be able to move on my husband's behalf. My husband then began to do what he needed to do as a husband and dad. This didn't happen overnight. In addition to our own efforts and actions, we had pastors, family, and friends interceding on our behalf. Don't just allow the enemy to attack you, your family, your friends, and your life. Take action! Pray, fast, praise, worship, and don't forsake (abandon, discard, reject) the fellowship of believers (church, pastors, elders, ministers) that can also pray, fast, and praise on your behalf. Don't be an island, alone and deserted by yourself fighting your battles. Involve other trustworthy believers who can fight the good fight of faith with you.

In due course, my husband and I were able to become unified, committing to God, diligently studying and applying the word, tithing, and going all-in for God. Once we were unified, we saw major breakthroughs in a short span of time. God began to restore and rebuild. We went from a one-bedroom apartment, to a townhome, to a nice home in a suburban neighborhood, which has more square footage and amenities than the home that we lost in foreclosure. We were also connected with pastors who prayed for us, sowed into us, and held us accountable. A few years later, my husband and I were even ordained in the ministry. During this time, we served God through working on our church's helps ministry team (volunteer efforts to assist in meeting the needs of the church and its members), we evangelized in the community, and we continued our journey. There were still ups and downs and periods of transition. As we faced challenges and obstacles, we made mistakes; however, we learned from those mistakes and kept and continue to move forward.

It has by no means been an easy journey. It's been a journey of growth, development, and healing. During hard times, God remained faithful, because God is faithful. Psalm 119:90 states that God's faithfulness extends to every generation, as enduring as the earth he created. When it looked like there was no way out of debt, not enough money for bills, relationships seemed unrepairable, and an unfinished PhD, God worked it all out. God made a way through reconciliation, job promotion, and meeting our financial needs. God allowed us to be restored from disarray, marital rifts, and brokenness. And God isn't done with our blessings! God made a way for me to finish my PhD when there wasn't enough money in the bank to pay for my last residency. God made a way to foster and repair relationships and build new, fruitful relationships. God was only able to do these things because we yielded to him and his will for our lives. God continues to meet our current needs, and he will meet our future needs and the needs of our future generations.

The principles that I've learned throughout my life, in my journey with God, from the Little White Church to where I am now, enabled me to "swim" and succeed when others thought it wasn't worth it, or that I would "sink". With God, my marriage overcame obstacles and challenges that the enemy tried to use to destroy it. As I think back over the years that God kept me in the fight, I realized that only a Strong Woman could endure and use those obstacles as a testimony for others.

There are five main characteristics that I feel helped, and continue to help, me make it through everyday life. In this mini-book, I share my perspective on these characteristics and their importance in being a Strong Woman. I think these characteristics are essential to the Strong Woman, for success as a daughter (to God and natural parents), wife, mom, sister, aunt, and friend. I also think that men can familiarize themselves with these characteristics, so they can better understand the innate qualities of women and how these qualities influence their roles as daughters, wives, moms, sisters, aunts, and friends. Understanding these characteristics can also enable men to begin to discover more about their innate qualities and walk in (live out) their God-given roles.

# 4

## WOMAN

Genesis 2:19-23—"Now the Lord God had formed out of the ground all the wild animals and all the birds in the sky. He brought them to the man to see what he would name them; and whatever the man called each living creature, that was its name. So the man gave names to all the livestock, the birds in the sky and all the wild animals. But for Adam no suitable helper was found. So the Lord God caused the man to fall into a deep sleep; and while he was sleeping, he took one of the man's ribs and then closed up the place with flesh. Then the Lord God made a woman from the rib he had taken out of the man, and he brought her to the man. The man said, 'This is now bone of my bones and flesh of my flesh; she shall be called "woman," for she was taken out of man."

When God created woman, she was created to be a "suitable helper." What is a suitable helper? A helper is simply one who helps. Webster defines help as "to give assistance, or support to; to make more pleasant." Suitable is having the qualities that are right, needed, or appropriate for something (able, capable, fit, good, qualified, competent). When God created woman, he had a purpose and a plan for her. Based on situations women encounter and go through, there is a tendency to forget that, in God's eyes, women are qualified, competent, capable, and have an innate ability to help. Many women, including myself, have struggled and gone through challenges, trials, and tests in life. Those challenges, trials, and tests should be used as tools for you to come out stronger and more confident in who you are in God. How can you have a testimony—testament, evidence, proof for others—if you don't encounter any tests? James 1:2 says, "Consider it pure joy, my brothers and sisters, whenever you face trials of many kinds, because you know that the testing of your faith produces perseverance. Let perseverance finish its work so that you may be mature and complete, not lacking anything."

Knowing that God created woman with intent and for a purpose should give you hope to keep moving forward and keep overcoming challenges that may seem impossible. The purpose of the subsequent chapters in this mini-book are to share with you, through biblical and personal reference, the practical (everyday, useful, concrete, feasible, doable, real) qualities that should embody (symbolize and represent) every woman of God. The obstacles, challenges, tests, and trials that you have gone through or are going through can be used to strengthen and develop these qualities, as you allow it.

# 5

## W-Wisdom

Job 28:12— "But where can wisdom be found? Where does understanding dwell? No mortal comprehends its worth; it cannot be found in the land of the living. The deep says, 'It is not in me'; the sea says, 'It is not with me.' It cannot be bought with the finest gold, nor can its price be weighed out in silver. It cannot be bought with the gold of Ophir, with precious onyx or lapis lazuli [precious stone, opaque gem]. Neither gold nor crystal can compare with it, nor can it be had for jewels of gold. Coral and jasper are not worthy of mention; the price of wisdom is beyond rubies. The topaz of Cush cannot compare with it; it cannot be bought with pure gold. Where then does wisdom come from? Where does understanding dwell? It is hidden from the eyes of every living thing, concealed even from the birds in the sky. Destruction and Death say, 'Only a rumor of it has reached our ears.' God understands the way to it and he alone knows where it dwells, for he views the ends of the earth and sees everything under the heavens. When he established the force of the wind and measured out the waters, when he made a decree for the rain and a path for the thunderstorm, then he looked at wisdom and appraised it; he confirmed it and tested it. And he said to the human race, 'The fear of the Lord—that is wisdom, and to shun evil is understanding."

As women and children of God, we should have wisdom. That is not to say we are knowledgeable on every subject; however, we should have and use wisdom in managing our lives. Webster's states that "wisdom is insightful understanding of what is true, right, or enduring; native (inherent) good judgment." The root/foundation of wisdom is "wise." According to Webster, wise is having discernment (insight): sagacious (marked by keen perception, clear sighted); sensible: prudent (managing carefully, handling practical matters with sound judgment); Having awareness or information: knowing.

Now that we know how wisdom is defined both biblically and from a dictionary standpoint, how important is it to have wisdom? According to Proverbs 4:7, "wisdom is the principal thing; therefore, get wisdom and with all thy getting get understanding." This scripture lets us know that wisdom is supreme—unmatched, untouchable, ultimate. The New Living version of Proverbs 4:7 states that "Getting wisdom is the wisest thing you can do! And whatever else you do, develop good judgment." For something to be considered supreme, it is of great importance and high power: maximum or utmost. In God's eyes, attaining wisdom is of high importance. As women of God, we should strive to attain wisdom. So...how do we attain (get) wisdom? The answer is simple: being in righteousness with God (upright and in right standing with the Lord), which includes reverence of the Lord, and studying and meditating (thinking about and pondering) on God's word, which ultimately enables you to attain (gain possession of) true wisdom, centered on and around God.

In 1 Corinthians 2:1, 3-7, Paul is writing to the Christians in Corinth. One of the purposes of Paul's letters was to assist the Corinthians in learning that they could not make it without God. The Corinthians were going through fighting, corruption, and hardship. Doesn't that sound like what's been going on in the world news the last few years? The scripture states, "And I, brethren, when I came to you, came not with excellency of speech or of wisdom, declaring unto you the testimony of God... And I was with you in weakness, and in fear, and in much trembling. And my speech and my preaching were not with enticing words of man's wisdom, but in demonstration of the Spirit and of power." In this scripture, Paul points out that he did not speak with human wisdom. Human wisdom encompasses things learned in the world, like a formal education (i.e. college degrees). Paul states that he spoke with words of great wisdom—not from earth, but the wisdom that comes from God. The NIV calls it God's secret wisdom. Paul's wisdom from God is secret wisdom because it tells of God's wise plan to bring us into the glories of heaven. The plan, which was hidden in former times, when men of the world had no understanding of it. This scripture illustrates the fact that we must be in right/good standing (righteousness, decency, morality, honor) with God, to not only attain wisdom but to sustain and increase our wisdom. James 1:5 states "If any of you lacks wisdom, you should ask God, who gives generously to all without finding fault, and it will be given to you". In your quest for wisdom, you should first ask God and then begin to seek practical, real-world wisdom through educating yourself. There are many ways to educate yourself including reading the bible and books, as well as taking classes, seminars, workshops, conferences, webinars, and attending church services. Obtaining wisdom is an ongoing, continual process.

Once we have wisdom, what do we do with it? How can we use it? James 3:17-18 states, "But the wisdom that is from above is first pure, then peaceable, gentle, and easy to be intreated, full of mercy and good fruits, without partiality, and without hypocrisy. And the fruit of righteousness is sown in peace of them that make peace." The wisdom that God imparts in us should result in bearing spiritual fruits. This scripture refers to several spiritual fruits: purity, peace-loving, considerate, submissive, full of mercy, impartial, and sincere. If we, women of God, have received and are continuing to receive wisdom from God, we should be exemplifying and showing these fruits. There should be display of these fruits in our lives outwardly. By continuously displaying these fruits in our daily lives, in the world (at work, at school, socially, in the grocery store, within our families, among our friends), we are letting our light shine. Matthew 5:16 states, "Let your light so shine before men, that they may see your good works, and glorify your Father which is in heaven." By letting our light shine (displaying spiritual fruits as a result of wisdom) we can let the glory of the Lord be seen to the saved and unsaved. We can then work to increase and advance God's kingdom, all because of the spiritual fruits that we bear, as a result of connection with wisdom.

There are times in life where we may not have operated or acted in wisdom. There have been times in my life where I said things to people or acted in ways that were not wise and sensible. As a result, I had to repent and then apologize to the people affected and rectify those actions. There have also been times where I've made decisions that were not the wisest decisions. I gave a few examples in my highlights from my days in undergraduate school. An additional example of an unwise decision is cultivating friendships with people that don't have your best interests at heart. I've found myself in that situation more than once in my adult life. When we find ourselves in situations that have the potential for us to act or choose unwisely, and to take us out of character (away from being the suitable helper we were created to be) pause and don't loose your composure or act hastily. Take a moment to think about what the wise decision or choice would be, and then make that wise decision. One option may be removing yourself from people and/or situations that can lead you into making an unwise choice or decision. No situation, family member, friend, neighbor, co-worker, employer, cashier, or social media connection is worth you being unwise and possibly jeopardizing your future blessings.

# 6

## O- Overcomer

John 16:33— "These things I have spoken unto you, that in me ye might have peace. In the world ye shall have tribulation: but be of good cheer; I have overcome the world." In this scripture, Jesus lets us know that we are going to face tribulations (encounter hardships, adversities, obstacles, difficulties, afflictions, distresses, misfortunes, etc.); however, we should remain positive during these tribulations because Jesus overcame (conquered and dominated) the world. In other words, he defeated, conquered, and overcame the things of this world. The Amplified version states, "In the world you have tribulation and distress and suffering, but be courageous [be confident, be undaunted (fearless, unafraid), be filled with joy]; I have overcome the world." [My conquest (victory, triumph) is accomplished, my victory abiding (remaining, long-lasting)].

This scripture itself gives us insight into what it truly means to overcome. First and foremost, to be an overcomer you must go through and experience situations that may not be desirable. To overcome those experiences and situations, you must defeat and conquer them. According to Webster's, to overcome means "to prevail; surmount; to win victory over (as in battle or competition)." In acknowledging that we are often in battle with the enemy (satan), comes the realization that we are going to experience tribulations either directly (firsthand for ourselves), or indirectly (through people we know and/or love). During these times, God wants us to overcome and have victory over the situation and satan.

How important is it to be an overcomer? Romans 5:3-5 states, "And not only this, but [with joy] let us exult in our sufferings and rejoice in our hardships, knowing that hardship (distress, pressure, trouble) produces patient endurance; and endurance, proven character (spiritual maturity); hope and confident assurance [of eternal salvation]. Such hope [in God's promises] never disappoints us, because God's love has been abundantly poured out within our hearts through the Holy Spirit who was given to us." This scripture lets us know that when we encounter and overcome trials and tribulations, we strengthen our patience, which helps develop and confirm (assure certainty or validity of, authenticate) our character. Ultimately, we learn how to trust God more and more as we overcome trials and tribulations. Our hope and faith, in turn, become strong and steady. As women of God and as God's children, we should be striving to be overcomers as we mature as Christians.

Are you or do you know someone who may have

encountered or is currently dealing with any of the following trials and/or tribulations:

- Unruly or disobedient children
- Disloyal or false-hearted relatives, spouse, or friends
- Alcoholism
- Drug use or drug addiction
- Fornication
- Adultery
- Lustful spirit, pornography
- Loss of job
- Loss of home
- Repossession of a car, furniture, appliances, or other belongings
- Not making enough money to meet demands
- Depression
- Feelings of abandonment and loneliness
- Self-hatred, afflicting pain on oneself
- Unhealthy relationships, ungodly relationships
- Low self-esteem
- Sins of habit (i.e. profanity)
- Jealousy or envy
- Selfishness ("what about me" syndrome)
- Anger, rage
- Unforgiveness, miscommunication, non-communication
- Controlling spirit
- Bound by tradition?

If the answer is yes, you can be an overcomer. You may be

asking yourself; how can I be an overcomer during trials and tribulations? Or overcome issues from the list above? I'm here to tell you that God is bigger than all the above-mentioned trials and much more. If you allow him to be. 1 Corinthians 10:13 states, "the temptations in your life are no different from what others experience. And God is faithful. He will not allow the temptation to be more than you can stand. When you are tempted, he will show you a way out so that you can endure." Knowing that God is faithful [adhering firmly and devoted, loyal, steadfast, true, steady, consistently reliable, secure, infallible, unfailing] during tests, trials, and tribulations should strengthen your outlook and perspective on being an overcomer. God wants to see you through your tests and trials so that in the end you will have a testimony of his goodness and grace. Many of you have heard people say, "You can't have a testimony without a test." Revelation 12:11 states, "And they overcame [and conquered] him because of the blood of the Lamb and because of the word of their testimony [by the blood of the Lamb's death and by the message they preached], for they did not love their life [and renounce their faith] even when faced with death." Knowing that you have Jesus Christ on your side should give you the courage and stamina to overcome what you may be experiencing or encountering. Likewise, you should be able to encourage others and help someone else overcome the situations they may be facing by telling them about what you went through and how God got you through it. That's your testimony.

How do we overcome? What steps do you take to begin to overcome? Relying on and trusting God and his word and making sure that we have on our spiritual armor of God will help us overcome and conquer life's situations. Whatever situation you are going through, find a scripture in the Bible that talks about conquering that situation and begin to meditate on it—read it repeatedly and speak it out loud. This will help you to get God's word in your heart, as well as allow you to speak over the situation you are dealing with according to God's word, so that God can move on the situation.

Ephesians 6:11-18 talks about the spiritual armor of God. "Put on all of God's armor so that you will be able to stand firm against all strategies of the devil. For we are not fighting against flesh-and-blood enemies, but against evil rulers and authorities of the unseen world, against mighty powers in this dark world, and against evil spirits in the heavenly places. Therefore, put on every piece of God's armor so you will be able to resist the enemy in the time of evil. Then after the battle you will still be standing firm. Stand your ground, putting on the belt of truth [being truthful] and the body armor of God's righteousness [righteousness is being in good standing with God through morality]. For shoes, put on the peace that comes from the Good News [God's word from the Bible] so that you will be fully prepared. In addition to all of these, hold up the shield of faith to stop the fiery arrows of the devil. Put on salvation as your helmet [meaning you consider yourself saved in the body of Christ and have accepted Jesus into your heart and life], and take the sword of the Spirit, which is the word of God. Practice praying in the Spirit often. Stay alert and be persistent in your prayers for all believers everywhere." Ephesians 6:18 mentions praying in the Spirit, which is important in spiritual warfare. Jude verse 20 goes along with Ephesians 6:18 in saying, "But you, dear friends, must build each other up in your most holy faith, pray in the power of the Holy Spirit." Essentially, you must become strong in your most holy faith and let the Holy Spirit lead you as you pray. Rely on and allow the Holy Spirit to guide your prayers according to God's will. Keep in mind that allowing the Holy Spirit to guide your prayers can include praying in an unknown tongue, dialect, or language. 1 Corinthians 14:2 states, "For he that speaketh in an unknown tongue speaketh not unto men, but unto God: for no man understandeth him; howbeit in the spirit he speaketh mysteries." ("But if your gift is that of being able to speak in tongues, that is, to speak in languages you have not learned, you will be talking to God but not others, since they won't be able to understand you. You will be speaking by the power of the spirit" (The Way Bible Translation).) By utilizing God's spiritual armor and relying on the Holy Spirit, we can be overcomers. What we've read in Ephesians 6:11-18 gives us vital information on the essential elements of spiritual armor that are needed to fight, win, and overcome tests, trials, and tribulations.

For me personally, it took the full armor of God to overcome most, if not all, of my past challenges. No one is exempt from challenges. I've mentioned some of my challenges. A substantial challenge that I had to overcome was that of a failed business that my Husband and I had, which was located at Stony Point Fashion Park. Since the business that we had wasn't an anchor store, one of the anchor stores decided they wanted to offer the products that we had. Because of this, our lease was not extended, and we were forced to close the store. This situation was devastating because we were not at fault and had invested a lot of time, money and labor hours into our business. In addition to this challenge other challenges that I've been faced with and overcame include overcoming mild postpartum depression after having my youngest son, overcoming health issues that included the onset of high blood pressure from pregnancy, overcoming feelings of self-doubt, and overcoming feelings of anxiety and restlessness. To overcome these challenging situations, I had to put on the full armor of God, which included being a person of truth and integrity, as well as speaking the word of God over the situations, so that I could attain peace and operate in faith in the midst of the challenges. It took the full armor then and it takes the full armor of God now, to guide me in parenting two sons in today's America, business challenges, pandemic challenges, and the challenges that come up with overall life-balance. The enemy will use anything that he can to get you off the path of righteousness. We must remind ourselves that the battle is against the unseen in the spirit world and not in the natural (what is seen). Being an overcomer is a continual process. We must continue to choose to overcome daily.

    I want you to think about a book you have read or a movie you've watched that portrayed or displayed soldiers fighting (Roman soldiers or Greek warriors, like in the movie Troy or 300). These soldiers are equipped with their armor and ready for war. Now visualize yourself being equipped with the spiritual armor from Ephesians 6. With this armor, you should be able to be more victorious than any past or present soldier fighting for the world's issues. Immersing yourself in the word of God through reading, listening, or watching Bible-based television, living in obedience and righteousness, sharing the gospel (scriptures and Christian beliefs) with others, expanding God's kingdom, and believing and trusting in Jesus Christ are advantageous to you, as you "put on" your armor and be an overcomer. Our daily routines and schedules should include prayer, spending time in God's word, and putting on our armor. We shouldn't let life situations like jobs, career goals, educational aspirations, extra-curricular activities, laziness, parenthood, spouses, or household tasks prohibit us from spending time in God's word or fellowshipping with one another and going to church. By not letting life's situations prohibit, hinder, or stop you, ultimately you will become equipped and ready to combat the "fiery darts" (test, trials, tribulations) that you encounter. Strive and make up your mind today, that with God you will be an overcomer.

# 7

## M-Modesty

1 Timothy 2:9, 10—"Likewise, I want women to adorn [beautify] themselves modestly and appropriately and discreetly in proper clothing, not with [elaborately] braided hair and gold or pearls or expensive clothes, but instead adorned by good deeds [helping others], as is proper for women who profess to worship God" (AMP). Let's reread the scripture from the NLT translation: "And I want women to be modest in their appearance. They should wear decent and appropriate clothing and not draw attention to themselves by the way they fix their hair or by wearing gold or pearls or expensive clothes. Women, who claim to be devoted to God or love God, should work on being attractive based on good things that they do". Which can include helping others or acts of kindness."

Initially you may think this scripture is about clothing, hair, or jewelry; however, this scripture tells us that women should be cognizant (aware) and mindful of being modest (humble, not boastful, arrogant, or self-centered). Furthermore, being modest is applicable to all God's children—not just women. Modesty is defined as having or showing a lack of conceit or vanity; reserved and having self-control in speech, behavior, or dress; humbleness, lowliness, and meekness. These characteristics are also illustrated in God's word when talking about fruits of the Spirit, which are basically characteristics that a person should exude and display (see Galatians 5:22 for further study).

The concept of modesty has often appeared to be distorted. Modesty, as it pertains to women, doesn't mean that jewelry cannot be worn, that women should refrain from makeup, or that women should deny themselves from wearing the latest fashions. Modesty means that you don't have to be heavily embellished in jewelry or makeup, that your clothing doesn't have to be revealing or so tight fitting that every curve can be seen. Believe it or not, modesty can also include a befitting hairstyle, in an effort to represent God and yourself well. Being modest can aid in deterring unsuitable and/or inappropriate behaviors, which lead to unrighteous behavior according to God's word.

How important is modesty? In 1 Timothy 2:9-10, Paul discusses modesty. "And that the women would also pray with clean hearts, dressed appropriately, and adorned modestly and sensibly, not flaunting their wealth. But they should be recognized instead by their beautiful deeds of kindness, suitable as one who worships God" (TPT). This scripture isn't just referring to modesty inside of an actual brick-and-mortar church building; it is applicable to everyday life because we (Christians) are the church. Modesty should be shown through our deeds, like how we treat others. Instead of being preoccupied with your outward appearance, be concerned about doing God's will and good deeds that will exemplify and demonstrate your love and devotion to God. Being devoted to God and doing his will and what pleases him is essential in living righteous and progressing from being saved and a Christian to being a disciple (follower, believer, pupil) of God. Isaiah 38: 3 states, "Remember now, O Lord, I beseech thee, how I have walked before thee in truth and with a perfect heart, and have done that which is good in thy sight." The New Living Translation reads, "Remember, O Lord, how I have always been faithful to you and have served you single-mindedly, always doing what pleases you." Within this scripture, Hezekiah prayed to the Lord because he had been told by Isaiah that he would die. Because God heard Hezekiah's prayer in Isaiah 38:3, fifteen years were added to his life. The essence and epitome of acting in modesty (humility, meekness, tactfulness, respectability) is being devoted to God, focusing on his word, doing his will, and what pleases him. In doing so, we can escape satan's traps, which can lead to destruction and death. Being modest and acting in modesty can be a demonstration of our devotion to God.

How do we go about being modest and showing modesty? Be humble, show kindness, pray before making decisions. Some of you may be thinking, is it really that serious? Why, yes, it is. Proverbs 3:6 (NLT) says "Seek his will in all you do, and he will show you which path to take." This scripture reference directs us to involve God in everything that we do, as we go about our day. Stop and take a moment to ask God through prayer and hear from the Holy Spirit. If you have doubt on appropriateness, choose a suitable modest option.

Having a sisterhood type of mentality can help in the process of being modest and showing modesty. This type of mentality entails walking in love and respecting one another, as well as being able to give constructive feedback, if your sister isn't walking in modesty. Let's be real. We have all had our "sister girl" moments where we might have given a neck roll with our answer. We've also been at church when someone's outfit was showing too much (male and female). In some churches, it has been left up to the "mothers" of the church to address issues like modesty. If we are walking in love, then one sister should be able to have a discussion with another (including teens and preteens) if she isn't demonstrating modesty. There shouldn't be any offense or backlash because of one sister discussing an issue with another sister, especially in the body of Christ. In addition to a sisterhood type of mentality, you can do a self-check, as well as rely on the people closet to you. I often do a self-check before I leave the house. If there is something "extra" being exposed or seen, then I correct it before I leave. There have been times when I had to add a cami, extra padding, or change undergarments so that certain clothing was not see through. In a world where sex sales, it's important not to fall into the category of its ok, because it's socially acceptable. I also use my family in my modesty check. If my attitude or body language came across as borderline, I often ask the people I am going out with (my husband, mom, sister, friends) and they help me to keep it cute with modesty (my humility and my clothes).

Keep in mind that God holds us accountable for our actions. As God's children, we cannot let some situations slide by or only rely on Pastors and/or Elders of the church to address them. There may be instances when the Pastor or Elder doesn't address a situation. We, as believers, should welcome reproof (reprimand) and correction. 2 Timothy 3:16 states, "All Scripture is God-breathed and is useful for teaching, rebuking, correcting and training in righteousness, so that the servant of God may be thoroughly equipped for every good work." God's word is given to us to teach us what is true and to assist us in realizing what is wrong and what may need adjusting in our lives. It aids in straightening us out and helping us to do what is right. "It is God's way of making us well prepared at every point, fully equipped to do good to everyone" (2 Timothy 3:17, TLB).

Essentially, we should be walking in modesty and encouraging others to do so. We should welcome correction in all areas of our lives, including the area of modesty, so that we can develop and be who God has called us to be. In your daily living and in making daily decisions, try to bring the concept of modesty to your remembrance. Thinking and acting on modesty can be a help for you, as you strive to do what is pleasing and acceptable to God.

# 8

## A-Anointing

Isaiah 61:1—"The Spirit of the Lord God is upon me, because the Lord has anointed and commissioned me to bring good news to the humble and afflicted; He has sent me to bind up [the wounds of] the brokenhearted, To proclaim release [from confinement and condemnation] to the [physical and spiritual] captives and freedom to prisoners."

The preceding scripture lets us know that in order to be anointed (to have an anointing), two things must occur: (1) God must give you the anointing. (2) You must be filled with the Holy Spirit. God uses his Spirit, the Holy Spirit, to anoint. Webster's refers to anoint as "to choose by or as if by divine election." For someone to be divinely chosen or elected, it must be bestowed upon them (given or granted) by God, in which God uses the Holy Spirit to do so. Esentially, God uses the Holy Spirit to bestow the anointing on his children.

What is the anointing? The anointing is the Holy Spirit, which is God's spirit, which can come upon you (dwell with you and inside of you). Ezekiel 36:27 reads, "And I will put my spirit within you, and cause you to walk in my statutes, and ye shall keep my judgments, and do them." I John 2:27 states, "But the anointing which ye have received of him abideth in you, and ye need not that any man teach you: but as the same anointing teacheth you of all things, and is truth, and is no lie, and even as it hath taught you, ye shall abide in him." The Living Bible states, "But you have received the Holy Spirit, and he lives within you, in your hearts, so that you don't need anyone to teach you what is right. For he teaches you all things, and he is the Truth, and no liar; and so, just as he has said, you must live in Christ, never to depart from him." These passages remind us that having the Holy Spirit in our lives is essential and imperative. The Holy Spirit acts as our teacher, comforter, and helper. In daily living, we should rely on the Holy Spirit, as we fight spiritually to stay on the righteous path that leads to heaven. As Christians, we are works in progress, and not perfected works. God has designated the Holy Spirit to be our guide as we make decisions and encounter various situations and circumstances. To be an anointed Christian is to have the Holy Spirit present and active in your life. It is often the anointing that God has imparted within you that can break and destroy yokes (burdens, oppression, bondage). I've heard testimonies where it was the anointing that sealed a business deal, delivered someone from a near-fatal incident, saved a family member, got the new job, got the college degree, or restored unity amongst families. Personally, I've witnessed the power of the anointing transform my life and my husband's life. I've witnessed the power of the anointing transform the hearts of people who we have had to do business with so that the outcome was a favorable one for us. This includes court cases, conducting business matters for businesses that we've owned, surpassing others and getting promotions ahead of people who had been in the same position for years, and even finishing my PhD and having to negotiate certain doctoral terms with the school board. The list goes on. No Christian today, living in this present evil world (with police brutality, school shootings, national and international terrorist attacks, political issues, infectious disease outbreaks, etc.) should choose to live without the anointing (God's Holy Spirit).

How do you get the anointing, if you don't think you have it? When people or "things" are anointed, it means that there is a divine (heavenly) influence. When you accept Jesus Christ as Lord and Savior, by asking him to come into your heart and reign over your life, there is a transference of the anointing, God's Holy Spirit. This means that God places his spirit within you. God's spirit then dwells (resides) within you. 1 Corinthians 12:13 (TLB) states that the Holy Spirit has fitted us all together into one body. We have been baptized into Christ's body by the one Spirit and have all been given that same Holy Spirit. Regardless of our backgrounds, whether similar or dissimilar, we are all given the same Holy Spirit, when we receive and accept Jesus Christ as our Lord and Savior, also referred to as salvation. Romans 10:9, 10 (ERV) reads "If you openly say, "Jesus is Lord" and believe in your heart that God raised him from death, you will be saved. Yes, we believe in Jesus deep in our hearts, and so we are made right with God. And we openly say that we believe in him, and so we are saved". After salvation, the Holy Spirit begins to dwell in us the moment we confess (speak; say) that we are saved, ask God to come into our hearts, and believe it. Oftentimes when satan tries to lure you into sin, there is a "voice" within you that tries to dissuade you. This "voice" may tell you the consequences, repercussions, or what-ifs that would be a result of your actions. This voice can be attributed to the anointing (the Holy Spirit), which was imparted when you made confessions of salvation and committed your life to God. When satan is busy being a tempter, the anointing is at work to guide you and lead you on the path that God wants you to go.

There are multiple ways the terms "anointed" and "anoint" are used. I discussed having the anointing, or God's Holy Spirit, within your life. To anoint, which is the act of anointing something or someone, takes on a different meaning. To anoint is to consecrate a thing, meaning that it is devoted and set apart to God. There is an account in the Bible (Mark 14:3-8) where a woman anoints Jesus' head with oil. In this account the woman is consecrating (dedicating to God, declaring Holy) Jesus' head. Not only can a person carry the anointing with them, they can also anoint others in the name of Jesus. As Christians the anointing is a quality that you should be aware of and yield (surrender, concede) to in your life. The anointing can guide and lead you in every aspect and situation of your life. As you read the word (the Holy Bible), listen to the word, and spend time with God through prayer and meditation, you will begin to recognize and know the presence of God's anointing. As you continue to mature and grow in your personal "walk" with the Lord (in your daily living) one of your goals should be to let God's anointing guide you and keep you.

In addition to the anointing and having the Holy Spirit dwell within you, the Bible talks about speaking in tongues. 1

Corinthians 14:2 reads, "For he that speaketh not unto men, but unto God: for no man understandeth him; nowbeit in the spirit he speaketh mysteries." The Living Bible states "...But if your gift is that of being able to 'speak in tongues,' that is, to speak in languages you haven't learned, you will be talking to God but not to others, since they won't be able to understand you. You will be speaking by the power of the Spirit, but it will be a secret." Speaking in tongues is a direct result of being "baptized" (immersed) in the Spirit. For clarity, receiving the Holy Spirit at the time of salvation and being baptized in the Spirit are not synonymous. Speaking and praying in the Spirit (meaning your prayer is led by the Holy Spirit and not by your conscious thinking) can assist you in yielding to God's will and walking in the anointing God has given you. Speaking in tongues (talking and praying in the Spirit) is a way of talking and praying to God in a manner that satan can't understand. When you receive the Holy Spirit, you can also ask God for the utterance (sounds, wording) to speak in tongues. At that time, you can let the Holy Spirit rest upon you and begin to speak in tongues.

I remember when I received the Holy Spirit and spoke in tongues for the first time. During this time, I was visiting Richmond Christian Center where my mother in law attended, and at the end of service I wanted to go up for the altar call for baptism with the Holy Spirit, but I didn't. I continued to attend services at RCC and even invited my youngest sister. On the Sunday she attended, I remember making the decision to go up for the altar call for baptism of the Holy Spirit. The moment was surreal because I don't remember stepping past people, walking down the aisle, or walking up to the altar. As I stood at the altar, I remember looking to my side and realizing that my sister had also answered the altar call. That day we both received the Holy Spirit with the evidence of speaking in tongues. I remember feeling extreme emotion, tears, and heat, like fire was in my bones, as the utterances poured out. It was truly a divine connection. After this exciting experience, I continued to read my Bible, apply the word to my life, attend church, pray, and develop my relationship with God. That was over twenty years ago.

As you think about the anointing, understand that it is essential in being a Strong Woman. The anointing can strengthen you when you thought you were weak or unable to face a situation or circumstance. Praying in the holy spirit during your quiet meditation time can help to develop, grow, and progress you. I try to pray in the holy spirit daily, as well as when I am in situations where I don't know how or what I should pray, I pray in the holy spirit and it works out well. The anointing can not only be a help to you but can be a vehicle (a way) for you to help others through your actions and your prayers.

# 9

## N- Nurturer

Ephesians 6:4— "And, ye fathers, provoke not your children to wrath: but bring them up in the nurture and admonition of the Lord." The Living Bible reads, "And now a word to you parents. Don't keep on scolding and nagging your children, making them angry and resentful. Rather, bring them up with the loving discipline the Lord himself approves, with suggestions and godly advice." This scripture details the importance of being a nurturer.

What is a nurturer? According to the latter passage, the characteristics of a nurturer include the act of guiding, training, and bringing up in a loving manner. A loving manner is a manner that supports and encourages in the process of raising or promoting development (i.e. training, educating, fostering, developing, cultivating, improving, rearing). A nurturer is one that trains, cares for, and encourages to assist in the successfulness of something that is animate (living), a person. There is great importance placed on the role of being a nurturer. Titus 2:5 states to train (or nurture) young women "to love their husbands and children, be virtuous and pure, keep a good house, be good wives. We don't want anyone looking down on God's message because of their behavior." If a woman isn't an innate (inborn) nurturer, she can be trained to be a nurturer through God's word, as well as through mentoring. The opposite behavior of a nurturer is displayed in an atmosphere or setting that is void of nurture, which can include anger, resentment, animosity, hatred, bitterness, offense, wrath, aggravation, lackadaisical (careless, halfhearted), uncaring, unsympathetic, unkind, callous, and emotionless behavior. Many of these antagonizing behaviors are listed in Galatians 5:19-21. The Bible states that people who live a life that embodies these antagonizing behaviors will not inherit the Kingdom of God. You can become a nurturer, if you aren't already one, or strengthen your nurturing skills by making a deliberate effort to align your behavior, both your actions and reactions, to that of a nurturer. There are times in my past where I have reacted or responded to people, including my children, in a manner that wasn't as nurturing as it should have been. In those moments, if you are still in the situation, respond in the same way that I strive to respond: quickly catch yourself and change your approach to one of a nurturer. If the situation has passed, ask God for forgiveness and to help you not to act uncharacteristically in the future, and then restore the situation with the person (apologize, smooth it over, talk it out). This will enable you to be an example, in allowing the person to see what the behavior of a nurturer looks like.

    It is essential to practice characteristics of being nurturer not just for others but for ourselves. The Bible says envy, jealousy, and wrath are like rottenness (decay) of the bones (Proverbs 14:30, AMPC). These antagonistic and opposite behaviors of a nurturer can create and lead to negative effects on the body like body aches, headaches, high blood pressure, and many other sicknesses and diseases. Practicing and living the characteristics of a nurturer are essential to you and others. God created women to be nurturers to raise children in a home setting that would promote love and kindness, gentleness, as well as be a support system. These attributes alone can strengthen children emotionally, so they can strive to be the best they can as they grow and develop; ultimately children can develop into adults that are loving, God fearing, and productive in society. Not only did God create women to be nurturers of children, he created us to be nurturers toward others. Oftentimes other adults we encounter may need nurturing. Not every child has or is going to grow up in a nurturing environment. Likewise, not every adult woman is always going to have it together. If the characteristics of being a nurturer are practiced amongst both adults and children, then we can be encouragers and motivators for each other. Can you imagine a setting (church, city, world) where there is no wrath, anger, offense, or hatred? Wouldn't that be a great environment or great place to be? Well, creating that type of environment starts with you. I often remind myself that it starts with me. Nurture can be giving another woman a compliment or helping a woman through a tough situation in a nonjudgmental way. I try to give compliments, and show kindness to other women, even when they don't seem receptive. Your small act of nurture may be what awakens the nurturer in another woman, that may have been dormant. The next time you have a conversation with someone (your child, a child, an adult) practice the characteristics of a nurturer and see change begin with you.

# 10

# *STRONG W.O.M.A.N.*

The woman is important to God and needed in the world, not just for procreation but to be a cornerstone (foundation) in households, work environments, school systems, community settings, marketplaces, and more. Being a Strong Woman includes embodying the qualities of a virtuous woman. A Strong Woman is a woman of **W**isdom, an **O**vercomer, one of **M**odesty that possesses the **A**nointing, and is a **N**urturer. Often, we've heard references to Proverbs 31 for the definition of a virtuous woman, a woman who has a moral standard of doing good (honorable) and not evil, rising early when necessary to accomplish her daily responsibilities, is a hard worker, understands business, has class, prioritizes, is an organizer, planner, multi-tasker, dependable, consistent, doesn't have self-pity or discontentment (anger and unhappiness), speaks words of insight, aids her husband, and fears the Lord. Being a Strong Woman is a woman who has the characteristics of a woman, as described in this mini-book, as well as one of virtue.

Every day we are faced with both opportunities and challenges. As we embrace opportunities and face challenges, we must remember the qualities that God has placed inside of us, as Strong Women. Use these qualities to conquer challenges and obstacles and keep moving forward. As you progress and move forward, respect yourself, as well as others, and have self-confidence. Don't let challenges and obstacles diminish your view of yourself. Remind yourself that you are fearfully and wonderfully made in Gods image. Personally, I've faced many obstacles and challenges where I've wanted to quit and give up on the situations and on myself. There were times in my life when I didn't know "the how" of how it was all going to work out. In those times, I had to fully trust God. There have been times in the past, when I didn't know how the bills were going to be paid (yes, even with graduate degrees). In parenting, there were times when I had to pray and continue to be the nurturer God called me to be instead of yelling and scolding. I often see parents in public lash out at their children, using profanity and crushing their spirits in the process. Don't be this type of person or parent. That isn't how God wants us to handle raising and/or mentoring children. Correction and discipline are often needed in raising/mentoring children. Seek God for guidance and make sure that disciplinary actions are followed by nurture, discussion with the child about their actions/behavior, as well as the consequences of those actions and behavior. I've been faced with challenges in the workplace, challenges in marriage, and challenges with illnesses. During these challenging times, I didn't quit, which wasn't easy because I felt like quitting. Instead of quitting or giving up, I kept praying, fasting, and serving God. I reminded myself of the mighty God that I serve, I put on my armor, gave the situations over to God in prayer, and watched God provide and work it all out, even when other people thought I was foolish to do so. Let the story of Hezekiah from 2 Kings 20:5-6, be an example of how God can answer prayers through trusting him. In 2 Kings 20:5-6, when Hezekiah was sick and near death, he prayed to God and God answered. 2 Kings 20:5-6 reads "I have heard your prayer and seen your tears; I will heal you. On the third day from now you will go up to the temple of the LORD. I will add fifteen years to your life" (NIV). Just as Hezekiah prayed to God and God moved, you also must pray and remain devoted to God, even when it may not feel good or it seems like it's not working out. If God worked it out for me, God can and will work it out for you, if you trust him and allow him to. Whatever situations, challenges, and circumstances you are facing, I ask you to give it to God in prayer, read scripture that pertains to your situation, remain steadfast (unwavering), and watch God work it out.

    My prayer is that after reading this mini-book, women feel more equipped to be the Strong Woman God has called them to be, and that men can utilize some of the principles discussed (like attaining wisdom, overcoming, allowing the anointing in their lives, and nurturing when needed), as well as encourage and support women in their pursuit of being a Strong Woman. I hope that this mini-book has opened your eyes regarding what lies within you and the inner strength that you possess through God! I also want to encourage you, if you don't attend a church regularly, to find a local church where you feel comfortable and are able to grow and develop. Join and partner with that church.

This will help you and strengthen you in your journey.   God Bless You, Strong Woman!

Scripture references include but are not limited to KJV, NIV, ESV, TPT, and Amplified Bible Versions.

www.ingramcontent.com/pod-product-compliance
Lightning Source LLC
Chambersburg PA
CBHW062023290426
44108CB00024B/2764